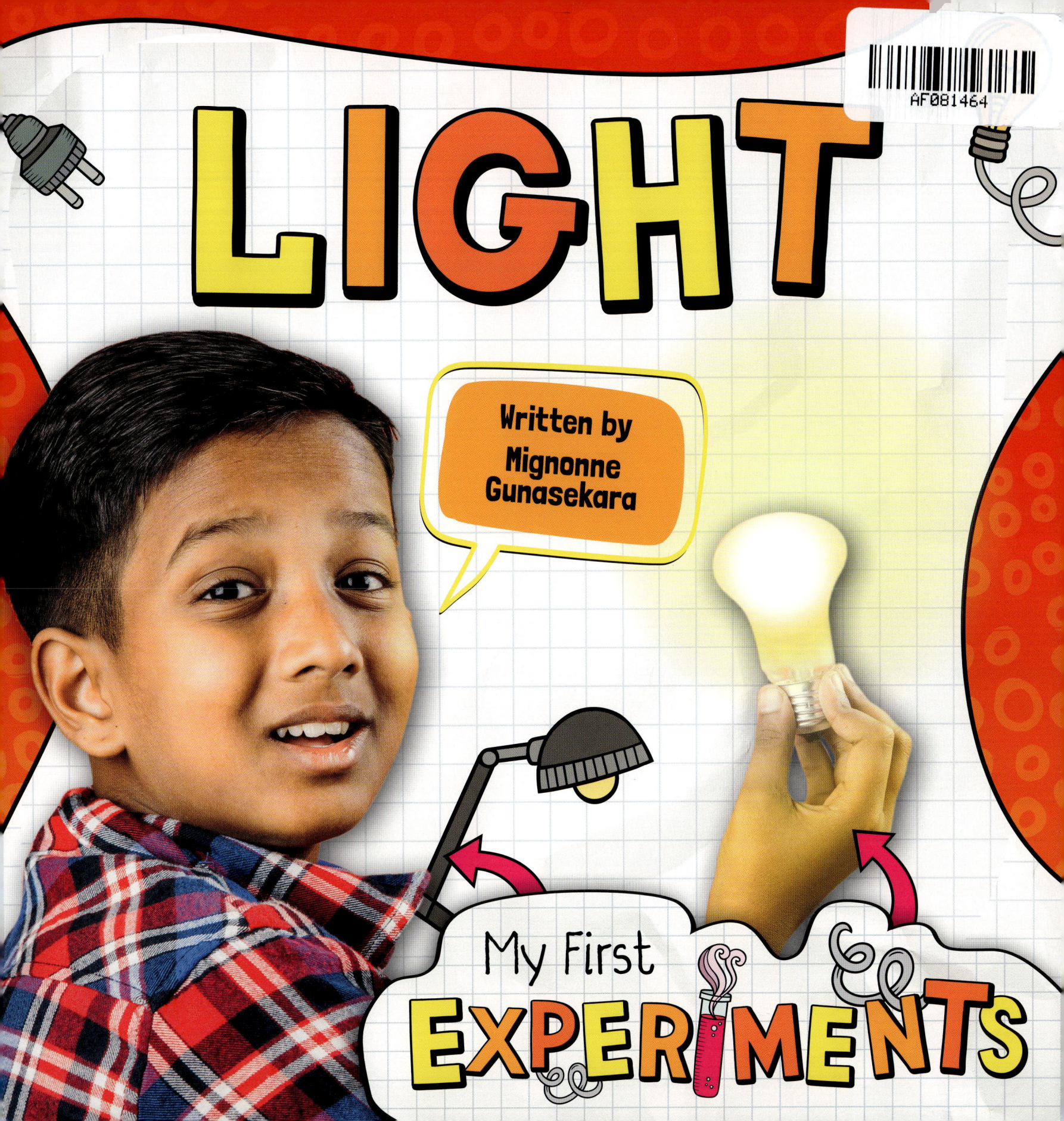

BookLife
PUBLISHING

©2020
BookLife Publishing Ltd.
King's Lynn
Norfolk, PE30 4LS

ISBN: 978-1-83927-121-2

Written by:
Mignonne Gunasekara

Edited by:
John Wood

Designed by:
Brandon Mattless

A catalogue record for this book is available from the British Library.

All facts, statistics, web addresses and URLs in this book were verified as valid and accurate at time of writing. No responsibility for any changes to external websites or references can be accepted by either the author or publisher.

All rights reserved. Printed in Malaysia.

To use the QR code in this book, a grown-up will need to set one of these apps as the default browser on the device you are using:
- Chrome
- Safari
- Firefox
- Ecosia

PHOTO CREDITS

Images are courtesy of Shutterstock.com. With thanks to Getty Images, Thinkstock Photo and iStockphoto.

Cover – LightField Studios, Serg64. Recurring Images (cover and internals) – ilkayalptekin (background pattern), The_Pixel (grid), balabolk (headers and vectors), wildfloweret (boxes), Steve Paint (arrows), yana shypova (speech bubbles), Tsaranna (vector frames and boxes). p4–5 – Mike McDonald, Vector Market, VaLiza p6-7 – Beautiful landscape, Dimedrol68, Rvector, Casezy idea p8-9 – Juergen Faelchle, PHILIPIMAGE, marina_ua p10-11 – RomeoLu, Triff p12-13 – Katie Flenker, Martynova Marina, rSnapshotPhotos, littlesam p14-15 – NeagoneFo, PR Image Factory p16-17 – udaix p18-19 – larryrains p20-21 – Gelpi p22-23 – Rawpixel.com

CONTENTS

Page 4	Hello, Scientists!
Page 6	What Is Light?
Page 8	Seeing Is Believing
Page 10	Let There Be Light
Page 12	Shifting Shadows
Page 14	Mirror, Mirror
Page 16	True Colours
Page 18	Experiment: White Light
Page 20	Experiment: Rad Rainbows
Page 22	The Badge Ceremony
Page 24	Glossary & Index

Words that look like this can be found in the glossary on page 24.

Hello, SCIENTISTS!

Science is about learning why and how everything works. A scientist's job is to find the answers to those questions.

LIGHT

Today, we will be learning about light. We will carry out a couple of fun experiments along the way.

After you've completed them, you will earn your Light Badge!

Let's learn about light!

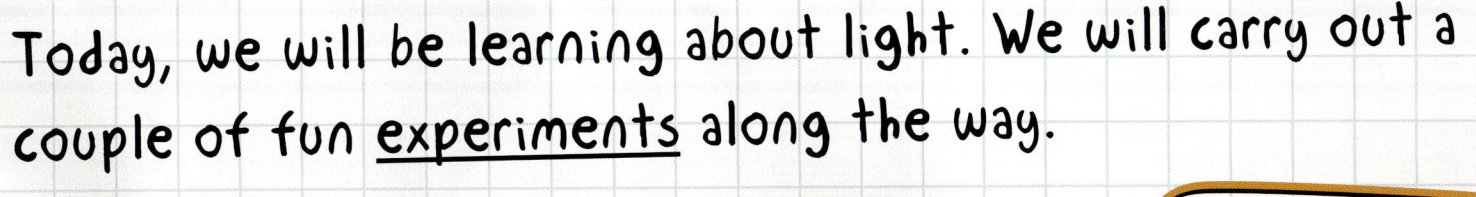

What Is LIGHT?

Light is what allows us to see. Without light, there is just darkness. Light comes from light <u>sources</u>. The Sun is our biggest light source.

There are many other different light sources, such as fire, torches and lamps. If we didn't have these light sources, we wouldn't be able to see much after the Sun goes down at night!

! You must not look straight at the Sun or other bright light sources, as this will hurt your eyes.

Seeing Is BELIEVING

Light comes out from its source in straight lines that never stop moving. Light moves so fast that it doesn't look like it moves at all.

Nothing can travel as fast as light.

The lines of light go into your eye through the pupil and hit the back of your eye. From there, your brain can draw a picture of what you see.

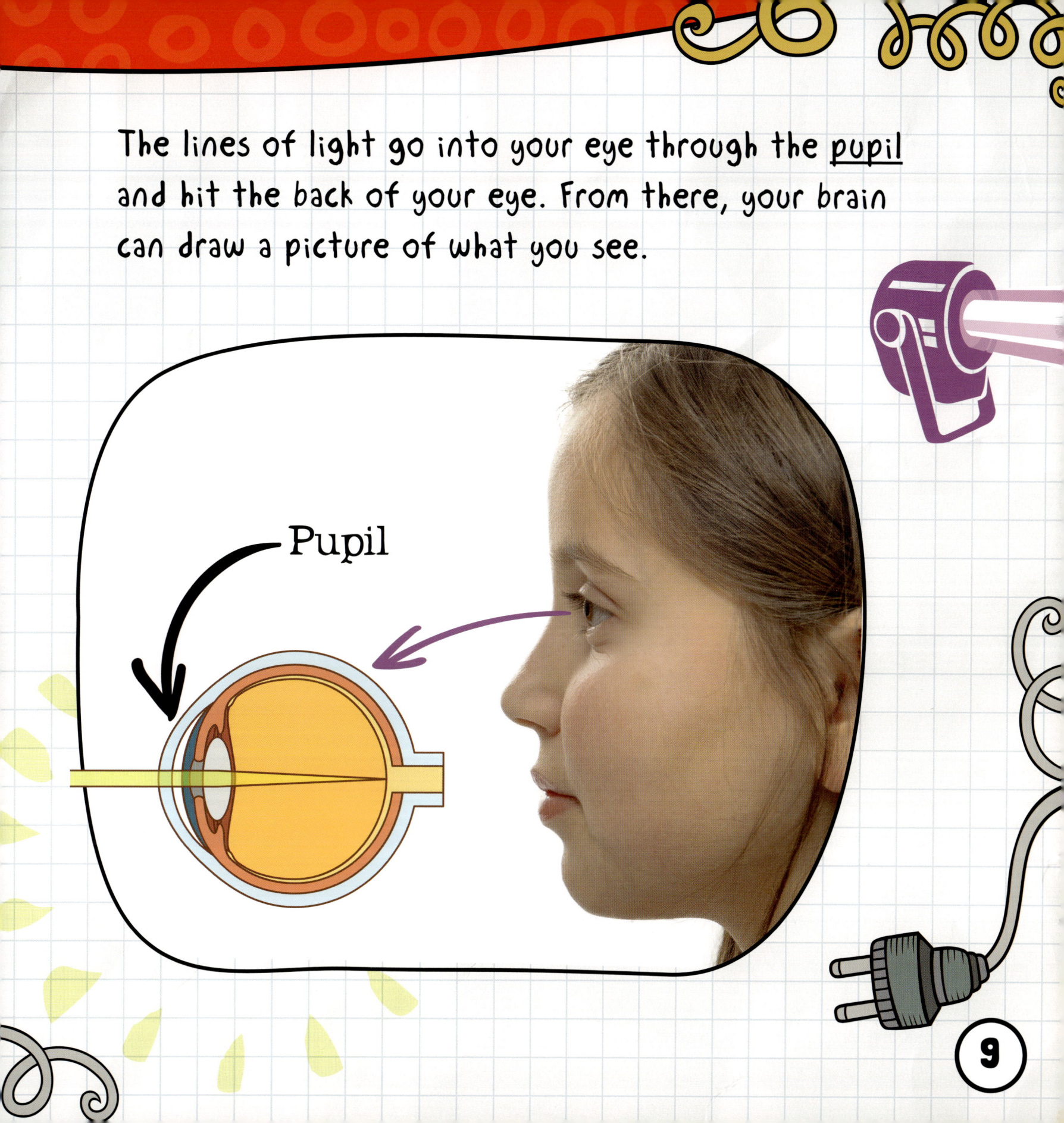

Pupil

Let There Be LIGHT

The Sun is a <u>natural</u> light source. It gives warmth and light for everything and everyone on Earth. It is very important for life. Without the Sun, there would be no living things on Earth.

Plants need sunlight to grow.

Electricity is a type of energy that can be used to make light. It can be used to power light bulbs. These are a type of human-made light source.

Energy is a type of power that can be used to do something. Examples include heat, sound and chemical energy.

Shifting SHADOWS

A shadow is made when light can't pass through an <u>object</u>. Objects that do not let light pass through them are called opaque. Objects that let light pass through them are called transparent.

The apple is opaque.

You can see through things that are transparent, such as glasses. This is because light can pass through them.

An object's shadow changes based on where the light is coming from and how far away the object is from the light source. For example, a tree's shadow changes as the Sun appears to move through the sky.

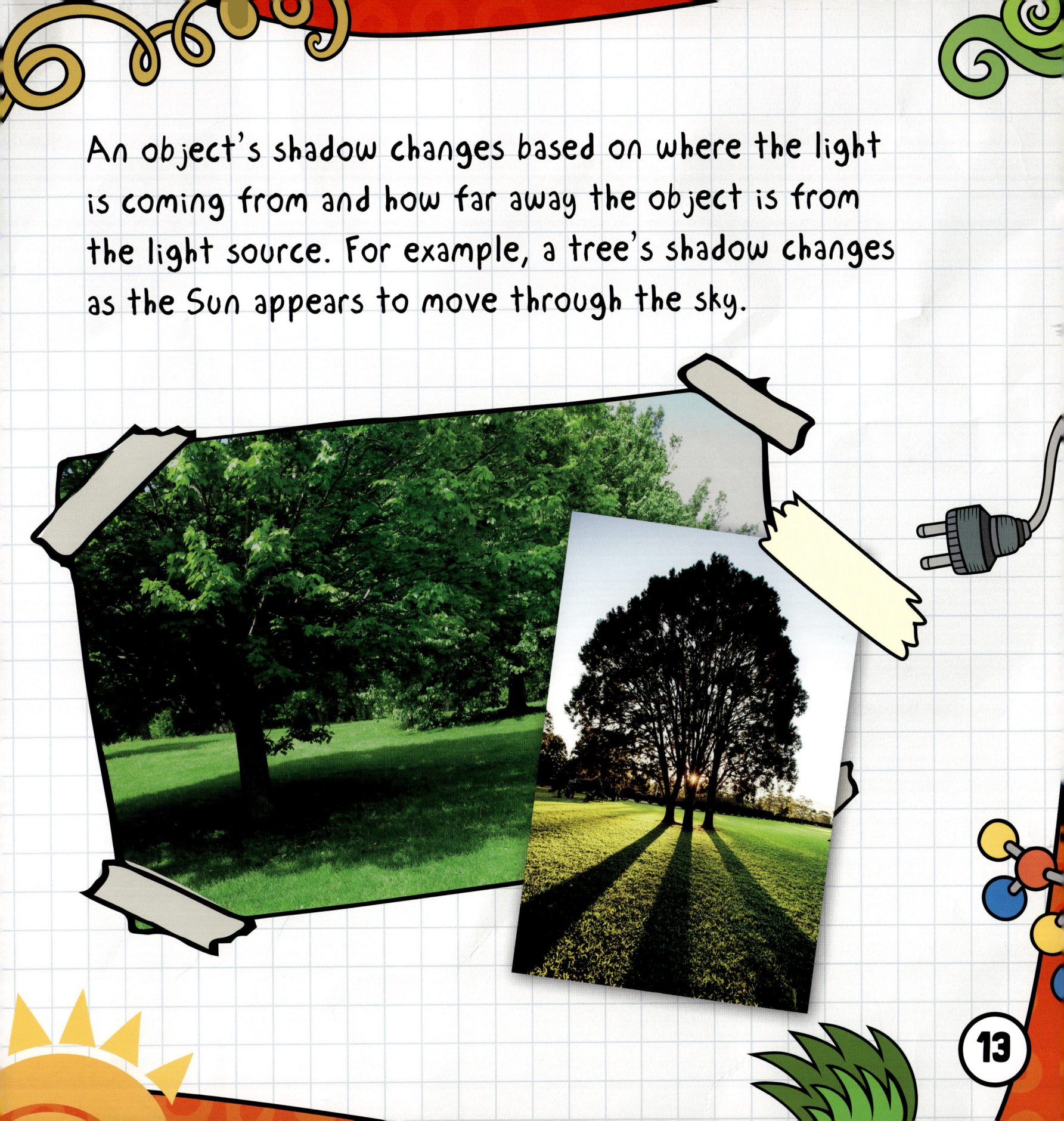

MIRROR, MIRROR

You can see things in a mirror because it is so shiny and smooth. Light bounces from an object to the mirror, and then into your eye. This is called a <u>reflection</u>.

The Moon is not a light source. But then how does it shine at night? The Moon can only be seen because it reflects the Sun's light.

TRUE COLOURS

Light comes in different colours. Different objects <u>absorb</u> and reflect different colours of light. If an object looks a certain colour, it is because light of that colour has been reflected and the other colours have been absorbed.

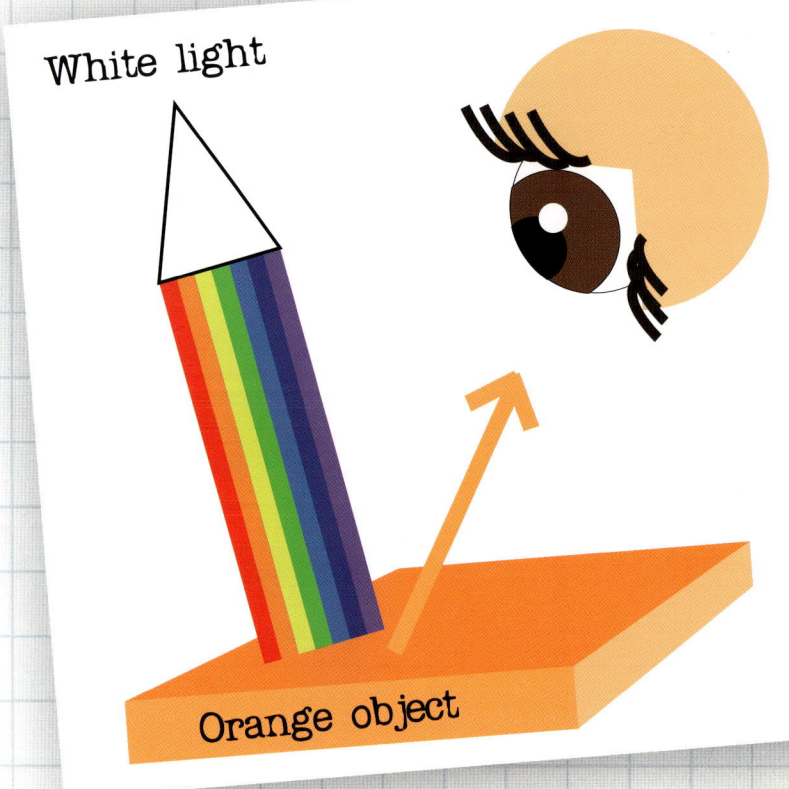

Only orange light is reflected by the object, so it looks orange to our eyes. The rest of the colours are absorbed.

The colours of the rainbow are red, orange, yellow, green, blue, indigo, and violet.

If an object absorbs all the colours of light, it looks black. If it doesn't absorb any light, it looks white. Sunlight is white light because it is full of all the colours of light in <u>equal</u> amounts.

How we see black

Black object

White object

How we see white

Experiment: WHITE LIGHT

Materials:
- A white paper plate
- Scissors
- Markers or colouring pencils in all the colours of the rainbow
- A sharp pencil
- A ruler

1) Cut the edges off your paper plate so that only the flat part is left.

2) Using the ruler and a pencil, measure around your plate and divide it into seven equal parts.

3) Colour each section in a different colour of the rainbow.

Ask an adult to help you with the scissors and the sharp pencil!

4) Poke the sharp pencil through the centre of the plate. The side you coloured in should be facing up.

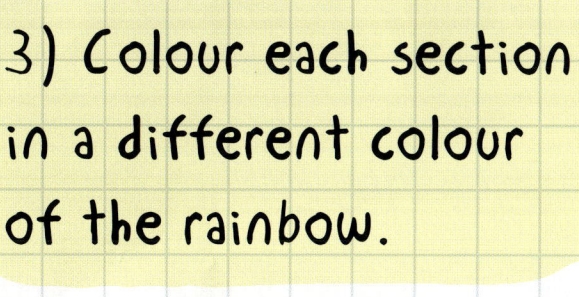

5) Use the pencil to spin the colour wheel like a spinning top. Spin it as fast as you can.

When all the colours are added together, they look white. Your wheel should look white when it is spinning.

Experiment: Rad RAINBOWS

In the last experiment, we looked at how the colours of the rainbow all added together look white. This time, we are going to break white light down into a rainbow.

Materials:
- A bowl of water
- A small mirror
- A sheet of white paper
- Sunshine, or another light source

1) Place the bowl of water in direct sunlight.

2) Hold the mirror halfway under the water, with the shiny side facing the sunlight.

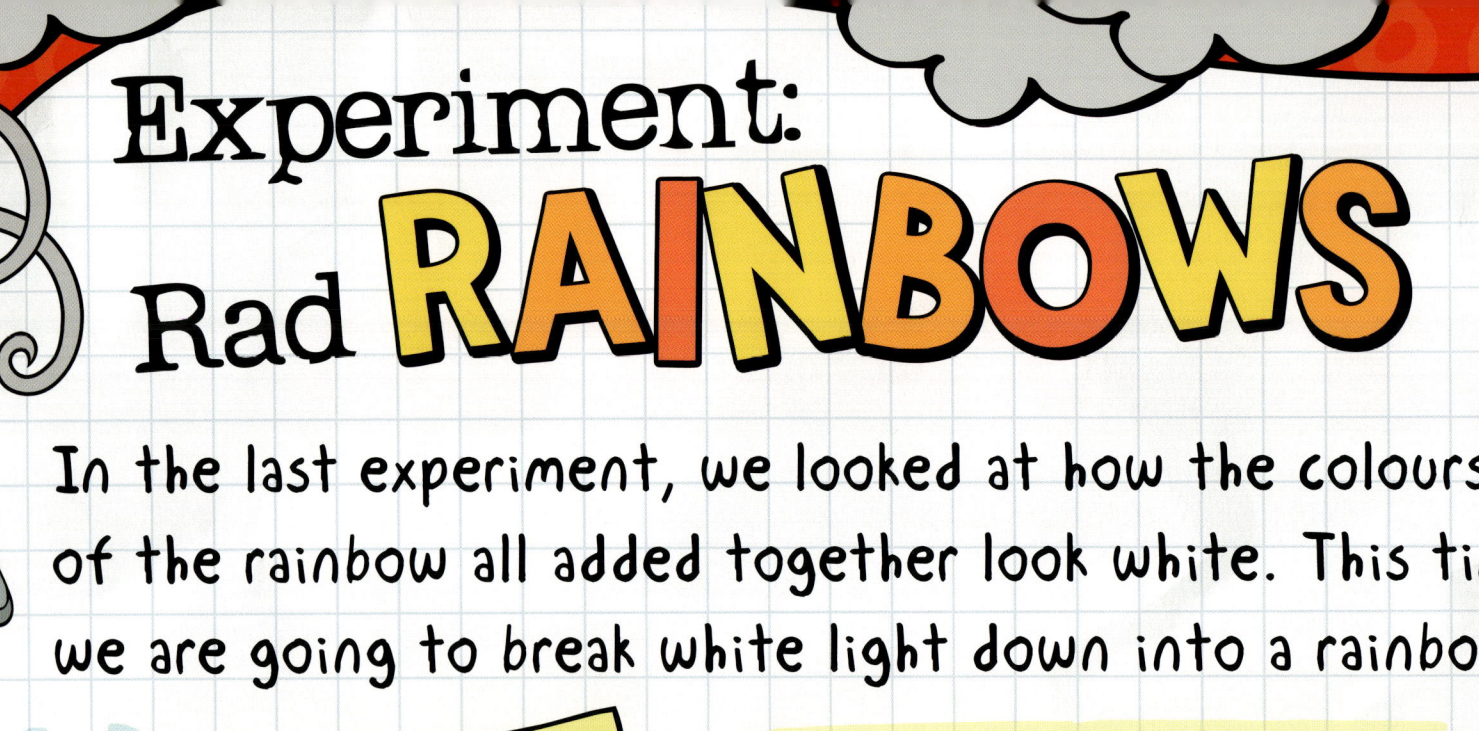

3) Hold the piece of paper up in front of the mirror, without blocking the sunlight.

4) Play with the angles of the paper and mirror until you see a rainbow on the paper!

There you have it – a rainbow!

The Badge CEREMONY

Well done for completing the experiments! Light is so interesting. We hope you enjoyed learning about it today. To celebrate, here is your Light Badge!

GLOSSARY

absorb	to take in or soak up
electricity	a type of energy that has many different uses
energy	a type of power, such as light or heat, that can be used to do something
equal	being of the same size or amount
experiments	tests done to explore and try new things
human-made	created by humans and not natural
natural	found in nature and not made by people
object	a thing that you can see and touch
pupil	the dark opening in the centre of each eye that lets in light
reflection	the bounce back of light, heat or sound
sources	where things begin or start from

INDEX

colours 16-20
electricity 11
mirrors 14, 20-21
Moon 15
objects 12-14, 16-17
rainbows 16, 18-21
reflections 14-16
shadows 12-13
sight 6-7, 9, 12, 14-15, 17, 21
sources 6-8, 10-11, 13, 15, 20
Sun 6-7, 10, 13, 15
sunlight 10, 17, 20-21